KT-873-069

The Making of a Champion

An International
Soccer Star

Ben Godsal

www.heinemann.co.uk/library
Visit our website to find out more information about **Heinemann Library** books.

To order:
☎ Phone 44 (0) 1865 888066
🖹 Send a fax to 44 (0) 1865 314091
💻 Visit the Heinemann Bookshop at www.heinemann.co.uk/library to browse our catalogue and order online.

First published in Great Britain by Heinemann Library, Halley Court, Jordan Hill, Oxford OX2 8EJ, part of Harcourt Education. Heinemann is a registered trademark of Harcourt Education Ltd.

© Harcourt Education Ltd 2004
The moral right of the proprietor has been asserted.

All rights reserved. No part of this publication may be reproduced, stored in a retrieval system, or transmitted in any form or by any means, electronic, mechanical, photocopying, recording, or otherwise, without either the prior written permission of the publishers or a licence permitting restricted copying in the United Kingdom issued by the Copyright Licensing Agency Ltd, 90 Tottenham Court Road, London W1T 4LP (www.cla.co.uk).

Editorial: Geoff Barker, Rebecca Hunter and Dan Nunn
Design: Ian Winton
Illustrations: Peter Bull and Stefan Chabluk
Picture Research: Rachel Tisdale
Consultant: Jim Foulerton
Production: Duncan Gilbert

Originated by Ambassador Litho Ltd
Printed in China by WKT Company Limited

ISBN 0 431 18935 8
08 07 06 05 04
10 9 8 7 6 5 4 3 2 1

British Library Cataloguing in Publication Data
Godsal, Ben
An international soccer star. – (The making of a champion)
1. Soccer – Juvenile literature
2. Soccer – Training – Juvenile literature
I. Title
796.334
A full catalogue record for this book is available from the British Library.

Acknowledgements
The publishers would like to thank the following for permission to reproduce photographs:

Empics pp. **5 top**, **5 bottom**, **6**, **8**, **9**, **20**, **21 top**, **21 bottom**, **22** (Mike Egerton), **26**, **27 bottom**, **28**, **29**, **30**, **31 top**, **31 bottom**, **32**, **33**, **34** (Tony Marshall), **35**, **38**, **39**, **40**, **41 bottom**; Getty Images pp. **4** (Clive Brunskill), **7 top**, **7 bottom** (SMG), **10** (Hamish Blair), **11** (Alex Livesey), **12** (Firo Foto), **13 top** (Shaun Botterill), **13 bottom** (Grazia Neri), **14**, **15** (Shaun Botterill), **16** (Gary M Prior), **17** (Phil Cole), **19 top** (Mike Hewitt), **19 bottom** (Alex Livesey), **23** (Liu Jin), **24** (Ben Radford), **25** (Stu Forester), **27 top** (Doug Pensinger), **36** (Laurence Griffiths), **37 top** (Jeff Gross), **37 bottom** (Shaun Botterill), **41 top** (Jonathan Daniel), **42**, **43** (Ben Radford).

Cover photograph reproduced with permission of Philippe Desmazes/AFP/Getty Images

Every effort has been made to contact copyright holders of any material reproduced in this book. Any omissions will be rectified in subsequent printings if notice is given to the publishers.

The paper used to print this book comes from sustainable resources.

Contents

Order No:

Class: 796·334 GOD

Accession No: 103342

Type: 3 WK

Words printed in bold letters, **like these**, are explained in the Glossary.

The global game

Soccer is the most popular sport on Earth. It is played by millions of people around the world – on green fields, tropical beaches and dusty roads. It is played by the rich and the poor, the young and the old, by men and women of every colour, religion and background. Football brings people together. You can go anywhere in the world – places where people speak a different language, eat different food or belong to a different religion – but say the word 'Beckham' and they will smile and understand. Soccer has a culture all of its own.

The journey

On 22 September 1976, a boy named Ronaldo De Lima was born in a poor neighbourhood in Rio, Brazil. Ronnie – as he was to become known – was brought up by his mother, a waitress at a pizza restaurant. Almost as soon as he could walk the young Ronnie spent most of his time playing football on the streets with his friends. As he got older, this worried Ronnie's mother, who wanted her son to spend more time studying. But it soon became clear Ronnie had a special talent. When he was thirteen he told his friends: 'One day I will become the best in the world.' At sixteen he scored his first goal for Brazil. Today many would agree he has fulfilled his ambition.

Life and death

The famous former Liverpool football manager Bill Shankly once said: 'Some people believe football is a matter of life and death... I can assure you it's much, much more important than that.'

Ronaldo wears the famous Brazilian number 9 shirt. He has come a long way since he kicked a ball around the streets of Rio as a child.

Japanese fans enjoy the 2002 World Cup, which was watched on television by billions of people around the world.

He is not the only one to think that football is more than just a game. When an important match is being played it seems to take priority over almost everything else. When Harold Macmillan became Prime Minister of the UK in 1957, the local newspaper in his home town of Brighton did not think his appointment was important enough for the front page – even though he had just been made one of the most powerful men in the world! Instead, the main story was a report about the local soccer club Brighton & Hove Albion.

Popularity fact

The last soccer World Cup in Japan and Korea in 2002 was watched on TV by nearly 30 billion people around the globe. More people watched the eight-week tournament than watched any other event in history. It was broadcast in 213 countries with each live match averaging a TV audience of around 356 million people. By the time the Brazilian Ronaldo scored to sink Germany in the World Cup final, more than a billion homes had switched on to watch.

African children play a dusty game of soccer. Football is popular all over the world.

How the game began

Soccer, as we know it, has only been around for about 150 years. The modern version was first played by boys at private schools and universities in England, which is why people think of Britain as the home of soccer. In fact, a similar sport was played over 2000 years before that – in China. The first ever game was said to have been played to mark the Emperor's birthday in 206 BC. Two teams had to kick a ball made of horsehair in between their opponents' posts. Legend has it that the winners were rewarded with a special feast while the losers had their heads chopped off.

The next stage

Versions of the game continued to be played with the rules changing all the time until the English Football Association wrote down an official set of rules in the 1860s. They have hardly changed since. The first league was set up in England in 1888 and was made up of 12 teams. It included famous clubs such as Aston Villa and Everton. Meanwhile the first game between two countries was in 1872 when England and Scotland played out a 0-0 draw in Glasgow.

England play Scotland in one of the first ever international matches, played in 1878. Here England are on the attack.

TOWER HAMLETS COLLEGE
Learning Centre
Poplar High Street
LONDON
E14 0AF

The early greats

As the game got older, skills and fitness improved and great players began to emerge from all over the world. There was the English striker Tom Finney who played in the 1950s and the spectacular Brazilian Pele. There was also Alfredo di Stefano (right, in white) who played for one of the most successful teams of all time – Real Madrid in the 1960s. He was a forward player who could pass, dribble and shoot with great skill.

Spreading the word

It was not long before the game began to catch on around the world. First it spread to countries in Europe. And then, as more people began to travel, so did football. One of the reasons soccer is so popular is because it can be played anywhere. It was also one of the ways European travellers kept themselves occupied when they were abroad. There was no television, but they could play football – as could anyone who happened to be watching... And so the game spread. By the time the first World Cup kicked off in 1930, football was the most popular sport on Earth. However, it was not until more recently that the game began to take off in places like the USA and Australia.

Into the modern age

Soccer in the 21st century is a very different game to that of 50 years ago. It is played by athletes who are fitter, stronger, richer and have more responsibilities than ever before. Women's soccer is also growing fast. The soccer champions of today have to work harder than ever if they are to get to the top.

England goalkeeper Margaret Turner (second from right) punches the ball away from danger in a match against Scotland in 1966. But women's soccer wasn't to take off properly until some years later.

Getting started

A great soccer player can pass the ball 30 metres to a teammate or trap it with one quick movement of the foot. He can score great goals and make crucial tackles too. But using these skills repeatedly throughout a football season takes a great deal of practice. Getting to the top in soccer takes a mixture of natural talent and hard work. Getting started is the easy part.

Taking the first step

Most of us kick balls around as soon as we can walk. Apart from soccer boots and shin pads, a ball is the only equipment a player needs. Great players of the past like Argentinian Diego Maradona first learned the game by kicking a ball around the streets of their neighbourhood. Uneven road surfaces meant the ball bounced off in funny directions, often making it difficult for the youngsters to control. But all that practice on uneven streets can eventually pay off. As players like Maradona have shown, a football star can start their career anywhere and still become a soccer champion.

You can start your career anywhere but with skill, hard work and a bit of luck you can still become a champion. Here, boys from Bolivia are taking their first steps to try to become the soccer stars of the future.

The ref

One person a professional game cannot survive without is a referee. The ref's job is to control the game. He does this by blowing his whistle when he sees a **foul**. If a player commits a bad foul the ref will show a yellow card. This is a warning. A second serious foul often means a red card, and the player can be sent off. A player can also receive a red card for committing a single foul that the referee considers to be particularly dangerous.

Camps and junior leagues

Young people from western countries are usually lucky enough to have an organized introduction to soccer. Some learn the basics at school. For others, holiday camps and youth leagues exist to give keen young players their early training. In Australia and the USA, soccer camps are run during holidays where boys and girls can develop their skills. There are also leagues in cities all over the USA run by the American Youth Soccer Organization (AYSO). Here kids as young as four are taught the game by coaches and volunteers. They learn training and fitness techniques but are also encouraged to enjoy themselves.

Boots fact

Soccer boots have come a long way since the early days. Back at the beginning of the 20th century, boots weighed 500 grams and became twice as heavy when it rained – so players were carrying around the equivalent of a bag of sugar on each foot. Now soccer boots are big business. Former Australian international and Liverpool player Craig Johnston realized that finding the right shape for a soccer boot would lead to greater ball control. After experimenting he came up with the Predator boot. The use of light materials and a shaped toe meant more swerve and power for shooting. The boot was made by Adidas and is now one of the most popular around.

Soccer boots have come a long way since the game began. Now boots such as the Predator are the right shape and weight, giving players greater control of the ball.

The art of attack

Being a great attacking player is about more than just scoring goals. Of course, all players love the glory of putting the ball in the back of the net but the best forwards (or strikers) have more to their game than that.

Key qualities

The best forwards all have the following qualities:

- Control: To get the team into a shooting position, a player needs to keep the ball close when running and be able to pass accurately to a teammate when the time is right.

- Confidence: Strikers are like all human beings, they need confidence to perform at their best. When a top forward stops scoring goals it is often because he has lost confidence.

- Cunning: A good striker will be clever. He will disguise his runs or the way he shoots so that the goalkeeper is kept guessing which way the ball will go.

- Team play: Most goals are a team effort. Teams usually play with two strikers and it is vital that they have a good understanding. Real Madrid pair Raúl and Ronaldo have scored many goals together. Often Ronaldo will create something with a piece of great skill while Raúl is a **penalty** box striker – which means he spends a lot of time inside the penalty box within range of goal. The two players complement each other perfectly.

Australia and Liverpool forward player Harry Kewell combines control, cunning, confidence and teamwork and is one of the top players in his position in the world. He is also very quick and creates as many goals for his teammates as he scores himself.

Raúl of Real Madrid and Spain is one of the best finishers in the game. In other words, when he shoots, he usually hits the target. He and his Madrid teammate Ronaldo work very well together as a strike partnership.

Scoring goals

Goals are scored in all sorts of weird and wonderful ways, from the simple close range tap-in, to the curling 30-metre screamer. Whether the ball comes off the head, the backside or the boot, the end result is the same. However they are scored, goals are what the crowds come to see.

Curling fact

When a player's path to goal is blocked by an opponent, he will often try to curve the ball around the opposing player. The secret behind curving or curling the ball is to hit it off-centre, which makes it spin through the air. It is not only forwards who need this skill but free-kick takers too. They often need to curve the ball round a wall of players in order to hit the target. Curling is a difficult skill which takes hours of practice.

Pulling the strings – the midfielders

Midfielders are like actors – they play many different roles. The best midfielders know how to defend, attack and do everything in between. They must also be exceptionally fit as they have to cover almost every blade of grass – chasing the ball down when the opposition are in possession, spraying passes and supporting the strikers when their team have the ball. Although players like Frenchman Zinedine Zidane can fill all these roles, sometimes teams give separate instructions to each midfielder so that the more creative players concentrate on attack while the best tacklers sit back and help with the defensive duties.

Zinedine Zidane

The French midfielder and 2003 World Footballer of the Year is still thought by many people to be the best midfielder around. Full of skill, the man they call Zizou is also extremely fit. He helped win France the World Cup in 1998 before taking them to the European Championship two years later. Zidane's French teammate Bixente Lizarazu once said: 'When we don't know what to do, we just give the ball to Zizou and he works something out.'

Passing the Brazilian way

Perhaps the most important string to the midfielder's bow is the ability to pass well. The Brazilian team have a long tradition of passing football. From players like Zico and Pele years ago, to modern day wizards like Rivaldo, Brazilians have always known how to pass the ball. Any player can pass the ball from A to B but a great passer must have variety, weight and disguise in his armoury.

TOWER HAMLETS COLLEGE
Learning Centre
Poplar High Street
LONDON
E14 0AF

The US star Claudio Reyna was one of the success stories of his country's impressive World Cup campaign in 2002. He is famed for his energy and neat all-round game.

- Variety is the spice of life... and passing. All players, especially midfielders, should be able to pass the ball to a player on the opposite side of the pitch or play a simple **one-two** with a teammate just a couple of feet away.

- Putting the right weight on a pass is also important. The ability to drive the ball hard into a player's path or chip it delicately for a teammate to run on to are signs of passing excellence.

- Perhaps what sets the good passers apart from the great ones is the ability to disguise where the ball is being played. Doing this can open up a gap in the opposition defence that did not seem to be there. England's David Beckham is a master at disguise. He may look like he is going to pass to one player but by cleverly changing the angle of his foot, he can send it to someone completely different.

Patrick Vieira, the Arsenal midfielder, is known for his tough tackling and phenomenal fitness. The tall Frenchman is a good passer of the ball too.

Solid as a rock – the defenders

While it is the skilful midfielders and goalscoring attackers who often claim the glory, a top team has its foundations in a solid defence. Defenders have to concentrate on doing the ugly – and sometimes painful – things well. They spend their time **marking**, tackling and heading the ball and will sometimes come off the pitch bloodied and bruised.

Defending as a unit

Although there are some great individual defenders, a team also has to work well together to defend effectively. There are two main types of defender: the centre back and the full back. Teams usually have two of each. The centre backs line up close to the goalkeeper and their job is normally to defend and guard the goal at all costs.

Catenaccio

Catenaccio was a cunning defensive system made famous by Italy's Inter Milan team of the 1960s and proved almost impossible to break down. It consisted of five defenders. Four of them stuck like glue to the four most attacking opponents, while the other was used as a sweeper, staying at the back and sweeping up anything missed by the other defenders. There seemed no way to break down

the system until finally the Scottish team Celtic – a side full of flare and creativity – unlocked the secret of catenaccio and won the 1967 European Cup (above). The Scottish team beat the Italian giants 2-1.

Offside fact

The offside rule was introduced to stop attackers hanging around their opponents' goal. It can be used by defenders to frustrate strikers who are not allowed to score from an offside position. A player is offside if he is nearer to his opponents' goal line than both the ball and at least two opponents – including the goalkeeper, and is actively involved in play. He is not offside if he is in his own half or if he is level with or further away from goal than at least two opponents when the ball is passed, or if he is not involved in the move in any way.

In the example on the left, the last attacker ⑨ is ahead of the defenders (in yellow) when ⑥ actually plays the ball. Therefore ⑨ is said to be offside.

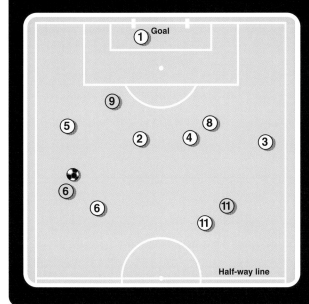

Full backs or wing backs take a position up wide by the touchline and have a slightly different role. They help out with tackling and marking but will also find space wide on the pitch so that their teammates can pass to them and an attack can be built. For a defence to work really well the full backs have to know instinctively when to help out the centre backs and when to go wide to launch an attack.

Roberto Carlos is an attacking full back for Brazil and Real Madrid. He has won everything from the European Champions League in 1998, 2000 and 2002 to the World Cup with Brazil in 2002.

Last line of defence – the goalkeeper

There is a long running joke in soccer that all goalkeepers are mad. Goalkeeping takes great physical and mental courage – which is probably where the goalie's reputation for craziness comes from. If an outfield player plays badly it will probably not affect the result of the match because his teammates can play well to make up for him. But when a goalie makes a mistake everyone sees it. Of course, saving goals is just as important as scoring them but goalkeepers are often remembered more for their mistakes than for the great saves they make.

Top tips for goalkeepers

The great goalkeepers of the past and present – Oliver Kahn of Germany, Carlo Cudicini and Francesco Toldo of Italy – all keep goal by the same rules. Former Scotland international and Arsenal goalkeeping coach Bob Wilson gives these guidelines for 'keepers:

• expect a shot or a cross at all times

• watch the ball carefully and stay behind the line of its flight

• catch the ball in a relaxed way

• when parrying the ball deflect it away at an angle

• call loudly to defenders when coming to claim the ball.

Woon Jae Lee of South Korea saves a penalty from Joaquim of Spain. Penalties are very difficult to save and goalkeepers can become heroes when they do prevent a goal.

Tim Howard

American Tim Howard is one of the rising stars of goalkeeping. Following in a rich tradition of US goalkeepers playing in England's Premiership (which includes Kasey Keller and Brad Friedel), the highly promising Howard was snapped up from New York Metrostars in 2003, where he had won Major League Soccer's Goalkeeper of the Year award for the second year running. Sir Alex Ferguson took him to Manchester United where Howard took the place of French World Cup winner Fabien Barthez. Howard's achievement is made all the more impressive because he lives with a serious condition. Howard has Tourette's Syndrome, a nervous disorder, but has learned to control it and says it doesn't affect his goalkeeping.

Narrowing the angle fact

The opposition striker is running towards you, your defenders are nowhere to be seen, only one thing stands between the onrushing striker and defeat – you the goalkeeper. These are the key moments of a game, the difference between winning and losing. So how can a goalie swing the odds in his favour? Top goal keeping coach Bob Wilson says he should come forward and narrow the angle, thus giving the striker a smaller target to aim at. He should also try and stay on his feet as long as possible, pushing the opponent as wide as he can. Hopefully he will then be close enough to block the ball.

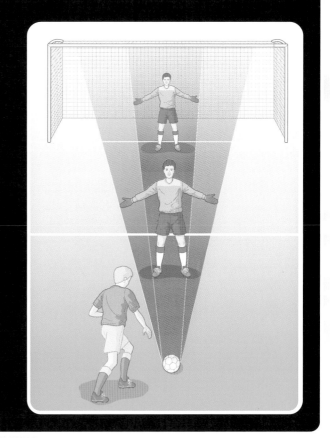

Champagne soccer

Nothing excites a soccer crowd more than a great piece of skill. The most exciting players are those who light up games with their magic. It is often those magical moments which stay in the memory long after the match result is gone and forgotten. A **back-heel** or **bicycle-kick** might not win a team the game but it certainly makes the price of a ticket worthwhile. These skills are also a great way of surprising opposing defenders.

Giggs on tricks

Ryan Giggs of Manchester United and Wales is one of the most gifted players of his generation. His range of skills has mesmerized spectators and opposing defenders for over a decade. The skills are learned on the training ground but being able to pull them off on the pitch comes down to talent and instinct. He says: 'All my skills are perfected on the training ground. I don't go into the game having decided to use a particular trick or skill, but if I can do one during the game it gives the crowd and the rest of the team a real lift.'

Cruyff turn fact

The Cruyff turn was named after Johan Cruyff, the great Dutch player of the 1970s who first used the skill. When perfected it can leave defenders for dead. This is how it works. The player looks as if he is going to pass the ball but instead drags it behind his standing leg with the inside of his foot. He then turns into the space left by the defender.

A moment of magic

When Giggs received the ball in the last minute of the 1999 FA cup semi-final against rivals Arsenal, there seemed nowhere for him to go. Twenty seconds of magic later, his team were through to the final. Giggs had picked up the ball deep inside his own half, run the length of the pitch, dribbled past six of his opponents and smashed the ball into the top corner of the net. The magician had conjured up a win from nothing.

Ryan Giggs of Manchester United celebrates after scoring a dramatic goal against West Ham in the fourth round of the FA Cup in 2003. A moment of flair and brilliance can sometimes change a match.

France's Thierry Henry is a master of the unexpected and the spectacular. Here the striker attempts to score for Arsenal with a bicycle kick.

Team play

A side can be full of talented players but they have to be able to play as a team. Each player must know his own job but he must also know how his job relates to what the rest of the team are doing. For example if a player misses a tackle, his teammates should be ready to cover for him. A side containing players of lesser ability can still be very successful if they stick together and work as a team. Ireland have reached the knockout stages of three of the last four World Cups even though they do not have the most skilful players to choose from. They did this through teamwork and organization.

Team spirit

A team with plenty of spirit has a distinct advantage over a team full of players who cannot stand the sight of each other. In order to trust teammates on the pitch, it is important that players respect each other off it. A team full of players wanting to win for each other is much more powerful than one full of players who want to win for themselves. Managers often say good team spirit can be worth an extra 10 points a season.

Glasgow Celtic doing their famous pre-match huddle. The players link arms to show that they will be playing as a team, give each other confidence and make every player feel like he belongs in the side.

Germany and the World Cup, 2002

In the lead up to the 2002 World Cup some experts described the German team named for the tournament as the worst national side the country had ever produced. They had been thrashed 5-1 by England in the qualification rounds. But by playing a disciplined game, closing down the opposition, making few mistakes and sticking together throughout the competition, Rudi Voller's side went all the way to the final where they met Brazil.

Voller knew he had less talented players to call on but still thought his side were in with a chance. Before the game he said: 'The best team does not always win, otherwise Brazil would have won it fourteen not four times. We know our strengths; we are well-organized, compact and have great spirit.' Eventually the Germans went down 2-0 but not before proving how far teamwork can get you.

The South Korea captain Myung Bo Hong, celebrates scoring the winning penalty, against Spain, during the quarter final of the 2002 World Cup.

Preparing to play – the boss

The role of the coach or manager has changed dramatically over the years. Once, the manager did nothing more than pick the team. Now he is probably the most important person at his club. A modern manager has to be a salesman, tactician, diplomat and motivator if he is to be successful. He has to buy and sell players, coax the best out of them and mould all the different personalities into a team. He also needs to outfox the opposing manager by choosing the right tactics to use. And if his team fails to fulfil expectations, the manager is the one who pays the price, by losing his job.

Sven Goran Eriksson

Sven Goran Eriksson is one of the best coaches in the world. He first made his name as manager of Swedish club Gothenburg before successful spells coaching Benfica in Portugal and then four different clubs in Italy's Serie A. He was a hero at Lazio where he brought them a league title as well as glory in the old European Cup Winner's Cup competition. In 2001 the Swede became England's first foreign manager. He is known for his knowledge of tactics and his ability to motivate players. England player Michael Owen says: 'There are no better managers around in the world. We are very lucky to have him. The players really respect him.'

Tactics talk

Before each match the coach decides what he thinks is the best formation to get the better of his team's next opponents. Sometimes he will use an attacking formation, sometimes a defensive one, depending on who his team are playing. There are three main systems: 4-4-2, 4-3-3 and 3-5-2.

- 4-4-2 is the most commonly used formation and is neither particularly defensive nor attacking. Here the manager picks four defenders, four midfielders and two strikers.

- 4-3-3 is a slightly more attacking system. It still includes four defenders but there is one less midfielder and one extra attacker. Teams will often switch to this system to give them an extra attacking option.

- 3-5-2 is the most fluid formation. In other words the system is easily adapted to the state of the game. It includes three central defenders, five midfielders and two strikers. Of the five midfielders, two are wide by the touchline. From there, they can make five defenders or become wingers (to make two extra attackers).

Stress fact

Managing a football club at the highest level is now so pressurized that coaches are being warned by doctors to watch their stress levels. In December 2001 Dave Bassett (then manager of Leicester) was wired up to a heart monitor during a Premiership game to test for stress levels. Bassett, then 57, said: 'It's a stressful job – but let's face it, lots of jobs are stressful.'

The coach has to communicate constantly with his players so the player can carry out his instructions. Here Real Madrid coach Carlos Queiroz chats to David Beckham during a training session on the ground.

Food and drink

A soccer player's diet is vital to how he performs on the pitch. Eating the right food and drinking the right liquids also greatly affects how quickly a player recovers from injury. You do not have to go too far back in time to find players preparing for a game with a greasy fried breakfast or traditional roast dinner! Smoking was also a common habit among players. But with the increase of scientific research players have now begun to realize the importance of healthy eating and healthy living.

The Wenger diet

When Frenchman Arsène Wenger joined Arsenal as manager in 1996, he was appalled at the eating habits of his players. He realized that with the right diet he could make his team fitter, stronger and less injury-prone than the other clubs in England's top division. Out went sugary foods, red meat, fry-ups and fatty dairy products and in came vegetables, fish, chicken and gallons of water. He even went as far as to give his players urine tests before each morning's training sessions. This way he could monitor how much water each of his men was drinking. And it worked too. That year, 1998, Arsenal won the Premiership and FA Cup double.

TOWER HAMLETS COLLEGE
Learning Centre
Poplar High Street
LONDON

Heat and humidity

The 2002 World Cup in Japan and Korea proved a real test for countries unused to the climate. Teams from North America and northern Europe were not accustomed to playing in high temperatures and humidity and had to arrive early to get used to the conditions. If players had been asked to get straight off the plane to play a match, they would not have been able to perform at anywhere near their best. This is because heat and humidity forces the heart to work harder. The body has to be trained to cope with this. American fitness expert Mark Higginbotham says that it takes two weeks in 26°C heat – and four when the temperature hits 32°C – for our bodies to get used to these conditions.

Italian player Fabio Cannavaro re-hydrates with a drink of water. It is vital for players to drink plenty of liquid before, during and after a match, especially in humid conditions.

Potato-power fact

After the 1996 European Championships French nutritionists criticized the diet of the England team. During the tournament the English players were living off soup, toast and spaghetti bolognese. They should have been eating potatoes! According to the experts potatoes are ideal for a pre-match feast. This is because they contain glucosides which offer a steady flow of energy to the muscles. They are also packed with vitamins. Ideally between 200 and 300 grams of boiled potatoes should be eaten around three hours before kick-off.

Fitness fever

To get to the top in soccer, players have to be ultra-fit. In order to be ready for the start of a new season, players spend more time working on their fitness than they do on tactics and ball skills. They have to be fit enough to play 90-minute games as often as 50 times a season. To reach these levels of fitness, coaches work out regimes for their players so that they can build up their strength, speed and endurance levels. These sessions may not always be a lot of fun but they are vital for team and player preparation.

Members of the England team jog during a training session. Speed and endurance running is practised so that players can last for the full 90 minutes of a match.

Speed endurance

Training should reflect a game: players need to last for 90 minutes so their endurance must be good. But soccer is not like long-distance running where athletes train so that they can pace themselves over a specific length of time. In soccer, players have to train their bodies for frequent bursts of speed. To be ready for this, teams spend a lot of time – especially at the start of a season – practising anaerobic or speed-endurance training.

Anaerobic training fact

A group of US college soccer players set out a programme designed to build-up speed endurance. Similar programmes are now used all over the world.

Running at about 90 per cent speed, players complete twelve runs of 15 metres each, followed by nine runs of 30 metres, and another twelve runs of 15 metres.

They have a short break (20 seconds) after each run, with a slightly longer break (2 minutes) after each set of three. After six weeks players should be able to complete every run at full speed. They then double their number of mini-runs so they have enough speed endurance to get them through a real match.

Extra time

A team's fitness is really put to the test when it is reduced to 10 men or when a match goes to **extra time** (which happens in **knock-out** matches when the game is still a draw after 90 minutes). England showed excellent fitness to last for nearly an hour and a half after Beckham was sent off in an epic game against Argentina in the 1998 World Cup. Here, Argentinian goalkeeper Carlos Roa saves a penalty kick from England's David Batty. The game went into extra time, finishing 2-2. Argentina won on penalties.

This involves a slow build-up of fitness in pre-season so by the time the first game kicks off players can not only last 90 minutes but also remain sharp throughout the game.

Warming up and warming down

Before and after every game or training session, players go through a series of stretching exercises. It is particularly important to stretch calves, groins and hamstrings as they can pull or tear quite easily. Stretching gets the body loose and warm before a game and allows it time to recover gradually afterwards.

England's Matthew Upson (left) and Wayne Rooney stretch their muscles. This loosens up the body before a game and helps prevent injury.

Recovering from injury

Today top professional soccer teams have a full medical staff complete with physiotherapists, nutritionists and club doctors. Football is such big business that clubs cannot afford for their top players to be **side-lined** through injury and will do anything they can to get a player back on his feet as soon as possible. Sometimes clubs are tempted to field players before they are ready, which can lead to further injury. As with all things, prevention is better than cure. And scientists say up to 75 percent of soccer injuries could be prevented if the right precautions are taken.

Ronaldo of Brazil was hurried back to fitness so he could play in the 1998 World Cup final. He was in hospital just before the game and should not have played. He made his injury worse and for the next three years played very few games.

Here are a few of the simple steps professional soccer players take in order to help them prevent injury:

- Warming up and warming down (see page 27).

- Having a sports massage. This releases the lumps and bumps in their bodies which are what cause muscle tears and strains. A few minutes on the massage couch can also help identify a potential long-term injury.

- Watching what they eat (see pages 24–25).

- Just being fit. A fit player is more likely to avoid injury.

- Having enough recovery time. Rest is vital. The body needs time to recover from hard exercise. Injuries often occur when a player pushes too hard.

Common injuries and recognizing the signs

The most common soccer injuries are groin strains, pulled hamstrings, cruciate ligament injuries, sprained ankles and shin splints. The most serious are broken legs, which can lead to a player's career ending. It is important for players to know when they are injured and to do something about it as quickly as possible. Hot spots on the skin, pain, stiffness, swelling and puffiness are signs that something might be wrong.

Former Nottingham Forest, West Ham United and England player Stuart Pearce broke his leg during a game. He was given a pain-killing spray while still on the pitch and attempted to play through the pain. He knew the injury was bad, but not that his leg was broken. By playing on, Pearce could have done himself serious long-term damage. Luckily he recovered but admitted he had been stupid to try to stay on the pitch.

Drugs in soccer

While football does not appear to have a major problem with performance-enhancing drugs, there have been a handful of cases in which banned substances have been found in players' blood. Players are given random drugs tests in which their urine is tested. If any player is found with drugs in his system he is given a long suspension from the game. Edgar Davids (right) of Holland and Fernando Couto of Portugal are two of the top stars who have been banned for drug-taking.

Emerging champions

The future of football around the world looks bright, with talented young players across Europe, Australia and the USA showing there is much to look forward to in the world of soccer. Football in Europe, South America and Africa has always been popular but many of tomorrow's soccer stars are likely to come from Australia, North America and the Far East, where the game is growing fast. And as soccer grows, so does the number of exciting young players.

USA paves the way

While soccer is producing players of immense talent from all over the world, it is young players from the USA who have been causing the biggest stir recently. Soccer in the USA is in a healthy state with more than three million young people attached to high school and youth soccer organizations. Girls' soccer is bigger in the USA than anywhere in the world, with women's national teams at U16 (under 16 years old), U17, U19 and U21 levels securing the future of women's soccer for many years to come – despite the collapse of one of the leagues in 2003.

Wondergirl

Lindsay Tarpley (right) is a young US soccer star destined for the biggest stage. The young forward is already captain of the US national U19 team and is a brilliant passer and fantastic goalscorer. Her greatest moment so far was scoring the winning goal against Canada in the final of the first ever World U19 championships. Lindsay is already on the fringes of the senior American team and was named US Soccer's Young Athlete of the Year 2002.

Wonderboy

Young American player Freddy Adu was just 14 years old when he signed a contract worth US$1 million with sportswear company Nike. Freddy, who plays as a striker,

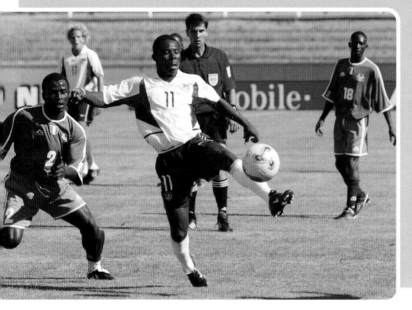

has scored lots of goals for every team he has played for. And even though he was just 14 he was already a regular for the US U17 national team. He also does not seem to get very nervous playing with people much older than him. In the 2003 Youth World Cup Freddy scored a **hat-trick**! He is now being chased by the world's biggest clubs, including Real Madrid and Manchester United.

Remember the name

There is no better place to spot future superstars than at the Youth World Cup. In the 2003 U17 tournament in Finland a few young players lit up the competition enough to suggest they could become the Beckhams of tomorrow. Brazil won the championships with defender Leonardo always impressive. Young Argentinian goalkeeper Oscar Ustari caught the eye with a string of top-class saves while one of the leading goalscorers was Colombian striker Carlos Hidalgo. But it was 16-year-old Spaniard Francesc 'Cesc' Fabregas who stole the show, scoring more goals than anyone else and picking up the best player award. (He now plays for Arsenal.)

Sweden's Jane Toernquist (right) tackles Germany's Maren Meinert during the women's 2003 World Cup final. The USA may be the home of modern women's soccer but Sweden knocked their American hosts out of the cup at the semi-final stage of the tournament. However, it was Germany who went on to lift the cup.

The women's game

Although the origins of women's soccer can be found in ancient times, it was not until the early 20th century that the game really took off. By the 1920s women's soccer was growing in Europe although most people did not consider it to be a suitable pastime for a woman. When a huge crowd of 53,000 turned up to watch a women's match in Liverpool it prompted an outrageous reaction from the English Football Association. The FA issued a statement banning women from playing saying: 'Football is quite unsuitable for ladies.' In China, women's soccer was more accepted. In fact it was being taught in schools as early as the 1920s.

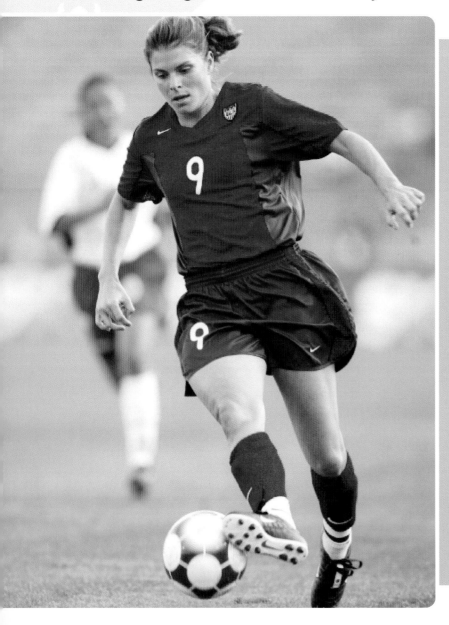

The greatest

One of the finest female soccer players ever to grace the pitch is US and Washington Freedom forward Mia Hamm. After sixteen years as an international player for the US team, Mia had scored a record-shattering 138 goals. She has a great **all-round game**; is a supreme dribbler, passer and finisher; and has won every medal going including the World Cup twice and Olympic gold once. And how does she do it? 'I think the most important thing with soccer is just to have fun with it,' she says. And what else? 'Practice, practice, practice.'

Going professional

In the late 1970s women's soccer really began to catch on. To begin with it was European countries that embraced the sport, with Sweden and Germany the most successful. But it was in the USA that women's soccer really exploded on to the sporting arena. A semi-professional league structure was set up in the late 1970s, since when the game has gone from strength to strength. Female players have commanded salaries of up to $85,000 for playing football. One league folded in 2003, but the Women's Premier Soccer League and W-League continue to grow. Other countries are following America's lead, with the sport beginning to emerge in Nigeria, Australia and England. A professional women's Premier League was set up in Japan in 1992.

A packed Pasadena Rose Bowl looks on as the USA play China in the final of the women's World Cup, 1999.

Women's World Cup

The first women's World Cup was played in China in 1991. The US team, nicknamed the Triple-Edged Sword because of the way they tore through the opposition, beat Norway in the final. Although Norway beat Germany to shock the Americans in the 1995 tournament, it was the turn of the USA again in 1999. They beat China in front of an astonishing 90,185 people at the Pasadena Rose Bowl in California. USA 2003 was again a tournament of upsets, with the US team surprisingly beaten by Sweden in the semi-finals. It was Germany who went on to lift the cup though, winning all of their matches and scoring 25 goals along the way.

It's all in the head

Soccer is not just about being fit and skilful, it is also about being able to handle pressure. When a manager wants to buy a player he looks as much at mental attributes as at physical strengths. In other words a top player has to be able to play at his best when it matters most. Any player who is fit and skilful can look good on the training ground but can he play well in an important match in front of thousands of people? Being able to do so separates the good players from the great ones.

The winning mentality

Coaches often talk about the need for their teams to have a winning mentality. This takes confidence, self-belief and above all team spirit. If a team goes behind late in the match it is natural for heads to drop, but a team with great spirit will often find a way of getting back into a game – even when it looks almost impossible.

David Trezeguet

When France beat Italy in the final of the 2000 European Championships, they were losing 1-0 as the game reached the 90th minute. French **substitute** Sylvain Wiltord nipped in for a last-gasp equalizer to take the game into extra-time. David Trezeguet (pictured right) then scored to wrap up a great win for France. After the game, French manager Roger Lemerre said: 'It is true we had our luck but it was the will-power of the team that won us this trophy.'

Shoot-out

There is no greater test of a player's nerve than when a match needs a **penalty** shoot-out to decide its outcome. This happens if a match is drawn even after **extra time** has been played. Five players from each team step up to shoot from the penalty spot at the opposing goalkeeper. The team who scores the most penalties wins the match. Without pressure, the odds would be heavily in favour of the penalty-taker. But for players responsible for winning or losing his team the match, the pressure can sometimes prove too much to bear.

Results may be important in professional soccer but fair play should never be forgotten. FIFA, the game's governing body, now gives out fair play awards to encourage teams to behave well on the pitch. The award is given to teams with the fewest red and yellow cards. In 2002 the Fair Play Award was given to the Belgium team.

Penalties decided the 1994 World Cup final and it was Italian striker Roberto Baggio who missed the crucial kick. Brazil won and Baggio was never the same player again. His confidence was shattered.

Big leagues and continental champs

While there can be no greater thrill for a player than to pull on the colours of his country, it is the club that provides the bread and butter of a professional soccer player's life. A player represents his club week in, week out and it is his club that picks up the wage bill at the end of each month. These days some club competitions – especially in Europe – are almost as important as international tournaments. While the most prestigious leagues – the English Premiership, La Liga in Spain, the German Bundesliga and the Italian Serie A – are considered the most important, the leagues in Japan, Australia and especially the USA are beginning to grow in significance.

Paolo Maldini of AC Milan holds aloft the trophy after winning the UEFA Champions League Final against Juventus in 2003.

The Champions League

The UEFA Champions League is the richest club competition in the world. TV companies pay huge amounts for the right to show matches. The league brings together the best club teams in Europe such as AC Milan, Bayern Munich and Real Madrid. The teams are split into mini-leagues with the top teams from each league going through to the quarter finals. The winners take home the European Cup.

Preparing for major championships

The World Cup is not the only major international event of the soccer calendar. Players also play for their countries in continental championships such as the African Nations Cup, European Championships and Copa America. Before they can compete in a major championship they have to qualify.

Major League Soccer

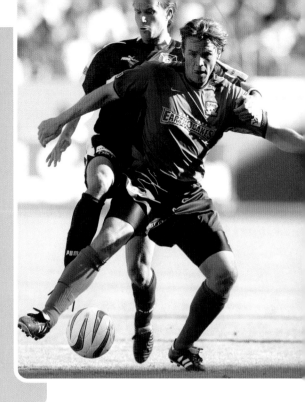

One of the conditions given to the USA before they hosted the 1994 World Cup was that the country should set up a national soccer league. By 1996 Major League Soccer (MLS) was up and running. The competition is very popular and gets bigger and better with every season. The 2002 final was played out in front of 61,000 screaming fans at the Gillette Stadium in Foxboro, Massachusetts. Los Angeles Galaxy were crowned champions and soccer in the USA announced that it was here to stay. The league is now attracting highly rated players from Europe and South America and with crowds and TV revenue on the up, the future looks bright for MLS.

Countries compete in a series of leagues with the top one or two from each league going on to the tournament. After qualification the teams play a series of friendlies so the manager can decide on his best side. The coach should make sure these games are played in similar conditions to those his team will face in the championship. An international manager will usually have his whole squad (around 22 players) together for four weeks before a tournament to build up team spirit and to work on team play.

Hatem Trabelsi of Tunisia is tackled by Noureddine Naybet of Morocco in the 2004 African Nations Cup final. Tunisia went on to win the trophy in front of their own fans.

Crowning of a champ – the World Cup

Every soccer player dreams of playing in a World Cup. It is what makes the endless hours of fitness training and the cold mid-winter matches worthwhile. It is also an opportunity to become a household name around the world or to win a dream transfer.

History

The competition has become bigger and more important each time it is played (every four years). The first World Cup in 1930 was won by the South American hosts Uruguay. Since then, when just thirteen teams competed for the trophy, the game has exploded in popularity. In the 2002 World Cup, 32 teams battled it out for the game's biggest prize and, as with every tournament before it, reputations were made and champions crowned by the time the trophy was handed over.

The 1970 World Cup

The Brazil side that beat Italy in the memorable 1970 World Cup final in Mexico is thought to be the greatest team ever to have played the game. Packed full of flair and skill they were also better prepared than other teams – working together as a unit and baffling team after team in the process. In the final the Brazilian team included four of the best players the world has ever seen: Carlos Alberto, Jairzinho, Rivelino and Pele (centre). The **free-flowing** South Americans overcame heat, altitude and the defensive strength of the Italians to win 4-1.

World Cup fact

As Brazil prepared to take on Germany in the 2002 World Cup final, star striker Ronaldo revealed that his team were getting ready for the biggest game of their careers in a rather strange fashion. Instead of poring over a tactics board finding clever ways to break down the opposition, his team spent the evening playing bingo (lotto) and telling jokes. It worked too – they won the match 2-0.

The biggest stage of all

A few good performances in a World Cup can make a player or manager world famous but reputations can also be ruined by the tournament. Every player aims to be at the very top of his game when the World Cup comes around. El Hadji Diouf of Senegal dazzled the world in 2002 and Oliver Kahn was even better. The German goalkeeper won the Golden Ball award for best player in the competition.

On the other hand Roger Lemerre, who was a hero after coaching his French team to European Championship glory in 2000, lost his job after World Cup 2002. France were knocked out in the first phase of the competition and Lemerre's reputation took a beating.

Senegal player El Hadji Diouf made his name with a great performance against cup holders France in 2002. Just before this, Liverpool had paid £10 million to sign him up.

Into the future

Football is a truly global game. It is a way of life for thousands of people. Not just around Europe and South America – but now in Africa, Australia and North America too. The game offers a way out for talented players from the poorest parts of the world, people desperate to become the soccer champs of tomorrow. Now more and more money is being invested in the game, some is beginning to filter down to poorer countries. This money should ensure the future of the game – allowing it to thrive and grow for years to come.

African football

The great Brazilian player Pele predicted that an African team would win the World Cup – before the end of the 20th century. Although that did not happen, there is no doubt the prediction will come true sooner rather than later. There may be little money in African soccer but it is a place rich in talent. Players and teams from Africa are also making a mark on the world stage.

Cameroon were the first to make the world sit up and take note when they reached the quarter finals of the 1990 World Cup. Since then Nigeria, South Africa and Senegal have also burst onto the world scene.

The New World

Nowhere is soccer growing faster than in Australia and the USA. While the best players from these countries still play abroad, better leagues and improved facilities are making others think twice before going overseas. More players are now staying at home. This in turn persuades promising young players to stay put, and so the standard of football improves.

40-year-old Roger Milla (right) dazzles at the 1990 World Cup – African football had arrived.

The Socceroos

Australian soccer is growing fast. Latest reports suggest more young people are taking up soccer than than the traditional Aussie sport of cricket. The country's governing body Soccer Australia has taken the game on in leaps and bounds. A national league has been set up which is slowly attracting better players, bigger sponsorship and more money. The Socceroos also boast world-class players such as Mark Viduka, Brett Emerton and Harry Kewell, and have recently recorded wins against top opposition, including England. For the game to take off even more, the national team must qualify for the World Cup – something they have managed only once in their history.

Brett Emerton of Australia and Blackburn Rovers scored Australia's third goal in their friendly match against England at Upton Park in 2003.

Major League Soccer is getting better and better. There are now a number of good teams including Columbus Crew and Chicago Fire – who can be seen battling it out on the left, in a match in 2003. Here, defender Nelson Akwari (left) of Columbus steals the ball from Chicago forward Nate Jaqua.

The modern soccer star

Being a top soccer player today is hard work but rewarding. Those who get to the top can be richly rewarded but it is a short career. Most professionals are able to play at a high level for about fifteen years if they are lucky. The top modern soccer players are like pop stars – rich and famous. But football is also demanding. Players work hard: they train for long hours and can be away from home for long stretches at a time.

Always on the move

Most professional players move clubs several times in a career, often to clubs abroad. They do this for all sorts of reasons. Sometimes clubs cannot afford to keep hold of a player, sometimes players want to move to bigger clubs. International players also spend a lot of time away with their countries – especially when a major championship is being played. At times all this moving can put a bit of a strain on family life but players do at least get to see the world!

Win some, lose some

Soccer stars can win the adoration of thousands one day, bear the brunt of the anger of millions the next. England midfielder David Beckham is probably the most famous player in the world. He has a pop star wife, wears designer clothes and is admired by millions.

England football captain David Beckham stands with his wife Victoria, proudly displaying an award received from Queen Elizabeth II at Buckingham Palace on 27 November 2003.

TOWER HAMLETS COLLEGE
Learning Centre
Poplar High Street
LONDON
E14 0AF

Transfer fact

In 1905 Sunderland player Alf Common moved from Sunderland to Middlesborough for £1,000. At the time the newspapers could not believe a footballer could cost so much. In 2001 French star Zinedine Zidane became the world's most expensive footballer moving from Juventus to Real Madrid for £46 million. How times change!

George Weah (above) of Liberia and AC Milan understood what it meant to put something back into a game from which he made his living. Weah paid for his country's trip to the African Nations Cup.

After the 1998 World Cup, things were very different. Soccer fans in England blamed Beckham when their country was knocked out of the World Cup. Beckham had been sent off in a crucial match against Argentina. The press and public hated him. Hardly a day went by when the newspapers did not carry a story about his private life. The pressures of his lifestyle would have been unbearable to most people. But after a lot of hard work on and off the pitch, he is now perhaps the best loved celebrity in Britain. Three years after Beckham's sending off, he scored the vital last-minute goal which won his country qualification to the 2002 World Cup. His transformation was complete.

Putting something back

It may be hard work sometimes but soccer players are lucky. They are paid for doing something they love. Most players try and put something back into the community – perhaps by visiting hospitals or donating money to good causes. Liberian footballer George Weah, one of the world's best players in the 1990s, was also a very generous man. When he discovered his country did not have enough money to pay for their trip to the African Nations Cup, he paid all their expenses himself.

Soccer records

Soccer players are no different from other sportsmen. They like to be the best and they like to break records. Fans like records too – it fuels the passion and pride they have for their clubs and countries. Below is a selection of records illustrating some of the game's highest achievers. There is also a run-down of a few of the key dates in the game's history.

World Cup Winners	
Team	Number of times won
Brazil	5
Italy	3
Germany	3
Uruguay	3
Argentina	2
England	1
France	1

Most World Cup Career Goals	
Player/Country	Goals
Gerd Muller, West Germany	14
Just Fontaine, France	13
Pele, Brazil	12
Ronaldo, Brazil	12

Recent World Footballers of the Year			
Year	Player	Club	Country
2003	Zinedine Zidane	Real Madrid	France
2002	Ronaldo	Real Madrid	Brazil
2001	Luis Figo	Real Madrid	Portugal

Key Dates in Soccer	
Year	Event
1862	Notts County becomes the world's first professional club
1863	English Football Association is formed
1874	Shinpads are introduced to protect players' legs
1875	Crossbar is introduced in place of the tape which used to run between each post
1925	Offside law is introduced
1930	First World Cup is won by Uruguay
1991	First women's World Cup is won by the USA

Amazing World Records fact

Pele scored more senior professional goals than anyone in history. The Brazilian scored a staggering 1281 goals in his career. He broke every scoring record in his country before becoming the only player to win three World Cups. In international matches he scored an average of one goal per game. In fact Pele probably holds the world record for breaking world records!

World Cup Records

Record	Result/Holders
Biggest World Cup finals win	Hungary 10-1 v El Salvador, 1982
Most World Cup appearances	Lothar Mattaus, Germany, 25
Most goals in a World Cup	Just Fontaine, France, 13, 1958
Most goals in a World Cup match	Oleg Salenko, 5, Russia v Cameroon 1994

World Football Records

Record	Result/Holders
Biggest international win	Australia 31-0 v American Samoa, 2001
Biggest crowd for a football match	Brazil v Uruguay, Maracana Stadium (World Cup final), Brazil, 199,854, in 1930
World's most expensive player	Zinedine Zidane, £46 million, 2001
World's most **capped** player	Hossam Hassan (Egypt 1985–2002), 160 caps

Country Records

English Records	Result/Holders
Biggest international win	13-0 v Ireland, 1882
Most international appearances	Peter Shilton, 125
Most international goals	Bobby Charlton, 49
Scottish Records	**Result/Holders**
Biggest international win	8-0 v Cyprus, Glasgow, 1969
Most international appearances	Kenny Dalglish, 102
Most international goals	Kenny Dalglish and Denis Law, both 30
Welsh Records	**Result/Holders**
Biggest international win	7-0 v Malta, Wrexham, 1978
Most international appearances	Neville Southall, 93
Most international goals	Ian Rush, 28
Northern Ireland Records	**Result/Holders**
Biggest international win	5-0 (twice) v Faroes, Lanskrona, 1991 and v Cyprus, Belfast, 1971
Most international appearances	Pat Jennings, 119
Most international goals	Colin Clarke, 13
Australian Records	**Result/Holders**
Biggest international win	31-0 v American Samoa, 2001
Most international appearances	Paul Wade, 119
Most international goals	John Kosima, 25
US Records	**Result/Holders**
Biggest international win	7-0 v El Salvador, 1993
Most international appearances	Coby Jones, 154 (as of 2003)
Most international goals	Eric Wynalda, 34

Statistics in this book were correct at time of going to press.

Glossary

all-round game
to be good at every aspect of the game (including passing, shooting and tackling)

back-heel
using a heel to pass the ball backwards

bicycle-kick
overhead-kick. A player with his back to goal hooks the ball over his shoulder to try to score.

capped
a player is awarded a cap, or capped, each time he plays for his country

extra time
time added at the end of a knock-out match so the outcome of the game can be decided

foul
mistimed tackle (can be deliberate or accidental)

free-flowing football
passage of play involving quick passing and keeping possession of the ball

free-kick
awarded by the referee after a player is fouled. The opposition have to be at least 10 metres away from the kicker, leaving him free to aim the ball in the direction he chooses.

hat-trick
when a player scores three goals in a game

knock-out
match or tournament such as the English FA Cup in which a team is knocked out if they lose a game

marking
a defensive player guards, or marks, an opposing attacker to stop him from scoring.

one-two
quick passing move between two players. One passes the ball, and the other returns the pass.

penalty
when a player is fouled inside the penalty-box a referee gives the fouled player's side a kick at goal. Only the shooter and the opposition goalkeeper are allowed in the box while the kick is being taken. The kick is taken from the penalty spot, 12 metres from goal.

side-lined (through injury)
when a player is not fit for selection

spread the ball
passing the ball long distances across the pitch

substitute
reserve player. Teams are allowed a number of reserves (either three or five) who can come on to the pitch in place of one of the players who started the match. Substitutes can be used for tactical reasons or because a player is injured.

Resources

Further reading

Go for the Goal: A Champions Guide to Winning in Soccer and Life, Mia Hamm (Quill 2000)
Inspirational story of the world's best woman footballer. The book includes useful advice for all budding female players.

Complete Conditioning for Soccer, Sigi Schmid (Human Kinetics 2000)
Concentrates on techniques for getting and keeping fit. Includes diet and injury advice, as well as warm up and training regimes for soccer players.

Women's Soccer: the Game and the World Cup, Jim Trecker (Universe Books 1999)
An account of how the women's game grew in popularity thanks to the World Cup.

The Sky Sports Football Yearbook 2003–2004, Jack Rollin and Glenda Rollin (ed.) (Headline)
Yearly compendium containing almost every fact and figure about the English game. Contains records, career statistics and past results.

Useful websites and addresses

Websites
www.womensoccer.com
www.footballculture.net
www.grassrootsfc.com
www.soccer.org
www.football365.com
www.planetfootball.com

Football federations

English Football Association
25 Soho Square, London, W1D 4F
www.TheFA.com

The Scottish Football Association,
Hampden Park, Glasgow, G42 9AY
tel: 0141 6166000
info@scottishfa.co.uk
www.scottishfa.co.uk

The Football Association of Wales,
Plymouth Chambers, 3 Westgate Street,
Cardiff, CF10 1DP
tel: 029 20372325
info@faw.org.uk
www.faw.org.uk

Irish Football Association,
20 Windsor Avenue, Belfast, BT9 6EE
tel: 02890 669458
enquiries@irishfa.com
www.irishfa.com

Soccer Australia
Level 3, East Stand, Telsta Stadium,
Edwin Flack Avenue, Homebush Bay,
NSW 2127
www.australiansoccer.com.au

US Soccer Federation,
1801 S. Prairie Avenue, Chicago, Il 60616
www.ussoccer.com

New Zealand Soccer (Inc)
PO Box 11–35, Ellerslie, Auckland
Tel: 09 525-6120
www.soccernz.co.nz

FIFA world football federation
FIFA House, Hitziweg House 11,
PO Box 85, 8030 Zurich, Switzerland
www.fifa.com

Disclaimer

All the Internet addresses (URLs) given in this book were valid at the time of going to press. However, due to the dynamic nature of the Internet, some addresses may have changed, or sites may have changed or ceased to exist since publication. While the author and Publishers regret any inconvenience this may cause readers, no responsibility for any such changes can be accepted by either the author or the Publishers.

Index

Titles in the *Making of a Champion* series include:

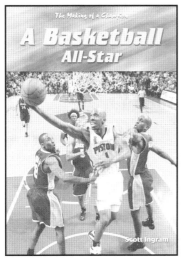

Hardback   0 431 18938 2

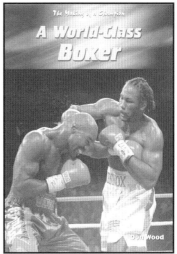

Hardback   0 431 18937 4

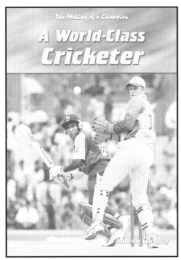

Hardback   0 431 18940 4

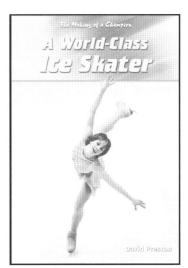

Hardback   0 431 18936 6

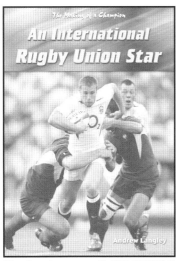

Hardback   0 431 18939 0

Hardback   0 431 18935 8

Find out about the other titles in this series on our website www.heinemann.co.uk/library